WHO GOES THERE?

1950'S HORROR & SCI-FI
MOVIE POSTERS
& LOBBY CARDS

volume seventeen of
the illustrated history of movies through posters

Previous Volumes:
Volume One: Cartoon Movie Posters
Volume Two: Cowboy Movie Posters
Volume Three: Academy Award® Winners' Movie Posters
Volume Four: Sports Movie Posters
Volume Five: Crime Movie Posters
Volume Six: More Cowboy Movie Posters
Volume Seven: Horror Movie Posters
Volume Eight: Best Pictures' Movie Posters
Volume Nine: Musical Movie Posters
Volume Ten: Serial Movie Posters
Volume Eleven: Horror, Sci-Fi & Fantasy Movie Posters
Volume Twelve: Comedy Movie Posters
Volume Thirteen: War Movie Posters
Volume Fourteen: Attack of the "B" Movie Posters
Volume Fifteen: Not Nominated Movie Posters
Volume Sixteen: To Be Continued…

D1127775

Edited and published by Bruce Hershenson
Published by Bruce Hershenson
P.O. Box 874, West Plains, MO 65775
Phone: (417) 256-9616 Fax: (417) 257-6948
mail@brucehershenson.com (e-mail)
http://www.brucehershenson.com or
http://www.emovieposter.com (website)

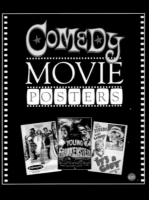

IF YOU ENJOYED THIS MOVIE POSTER BOOK, THEN YOU

ARE SURE TO ENJOY THESE OTHER SIMILAR BRUCE

HERSHENSON PUBLICATIONS. LOOK FOR THEM AT YOUR

LOCAL BOOKSTORE OR ORDER THEM DIRECT FROM

THE PUBLISHER.

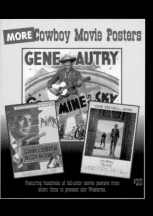

INTRODUCTION

Welcome to the seventeenth volume of the Illustrated History of Movies Through Posters. This book is different from the previous volumes in an unusual way. Almost all of the images in the previous volumes came from the archive I co-own with my partner, Richard Allen, the Hershenson-Allen Archive (the archive consists of over 35,000 different movie poster images, all photographed directly from the original posters onto high quality 4" x 5" color transparencies; There is not another resource like it anywhere, and it is the world's foremost source of movie poster images).

But almost all of the posters in this volume came from two collectors, both of whom built their collections over many years. One made an effort to get complete sets of eight lobby cards from EVERY 1950s (and early 1960s) horror/sci-fi film of note, and he did a pretty amazing job of coming close to reaching his goal! It is difficult to find ANY complete eight sets from 1950s films. Most of them were long ago split up and sold by the individual card.

The other collector sought out posters from the most important of these films, those with the most striking images. You'll find posters from most of the more memorable 1950s and early 1960s horror/sci-fi classics, as well as some from films that were not highly regarded in their day, but have achieved cult status over the years.

1950s horror and science fiction film posters have been far and away the most collected genre of film ever since the modern movie poster collecting hobby took root in the 1960s. Why should that be? One theory is that people collect what they remember most vividly, and certainly these films leave a deep impression on those who see them as adolescents! Another holds that this genre is so popular because of the wild and outrageous images on the posters, often far more interesting and appealing than the films themselves.

The vast appeal of 1950s horror/sci-fi is probably a combination of these factors. It is also worthwhile pointing out that, unlike every other genre of film, this genre literally began in 1950. While all other genres (cowboy, adventure, drama, comedy, horror, etc.) began at the turn of the century when film was first invented, there were really next-to-no science fiction films (with the notable exceptions of Metropolis and Things To Come). Perhaps this was because of the huge expense of special effects (and the lack of technology to create them), or perhaps it was because the few science fiction books that were written prior to 1940 were more fantasy than serious speculation on the future.

But World War II and the reality of atom bombs changed all that. A new breed of science fiction writers (led by Robert Heinlein, Isaac Asimov, and others) rapidly wrote many novels of realistic future speculation. But it was the UFO scares of the early 1950s that were the catalysts for the 1950s science fiction movies. Just about every film featured either monsters from "outer space" or monsters created by atomic radiation (and sometimes both!).

It seems that when men finally began to explore space in reality the great cycle of sci-fi films that had begun in 1950 started to wind down. Perhaps it was because scientific exploration had not turned up any "bug-eyed" monsters, or maybe it was just that the cycle had finally run its course. But those films left a wonderful legacy of outrageous poster art unlike anything that came before or after!

I need to thank Phillip Wages, Erik Bennett, Sean Burke, and Sylvia Hershenson, who assisted in the preparation and proofreading of this book. I also need to thank Amy Knight who did the layouts and designed the covers.

I dedicate this book to the memory of one of the first and greatest collectors of movie posters and lobby cards, Bob Scherl. Bob's knowledge of film was encyclopedic, and he loved movies more than anyone I have ever met. I always looked forward to visiting him, and seeing a couple of films from his vast library. I miss him very much.

Bruce Hershenson
June 2001

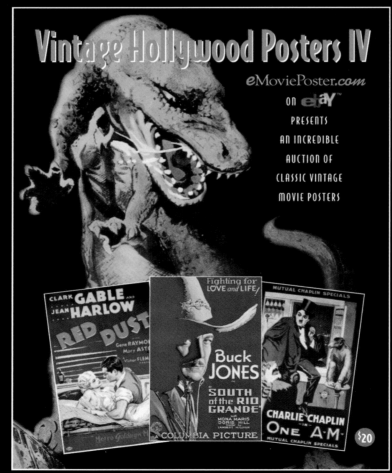

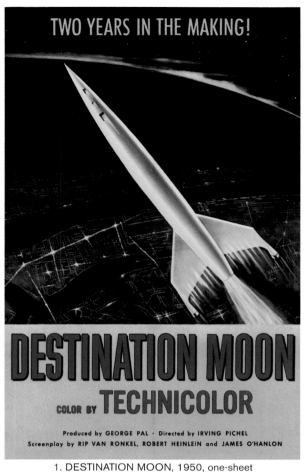

TWO YEARS IN THE MAKING!

DESTINATION MOON
COLOR BY TECHNICOLOR

Produced by GEORGE PAL · Directed by IRVING PICHEL
Screenplay by RIP VAN RONKEL, ROBERT HEINLEIN and JAMES O'HANLON

1. DESTINATION MOON, 1950, one-sheet

SHOCKING! A BLONDE BEAUTY and a SAVAGE BEAST...ALONE in the JUNGLE!

JACK BRODER Productions presents

Bride of the GORILLA

Starring BARBARA PAYTON LON CHANEY
RAYMOND BURR TOM CONWAY
Written and Directed by CURT SIODMAK

Bride of the GORILLA
Starring BARBARA PAYTON LON CHANEY RAYMOND BURR TOM CONWAY
Written and Directed by CURT SIODMAK

2. BRIDE OF THE GORILLA, 1951, lobby cards

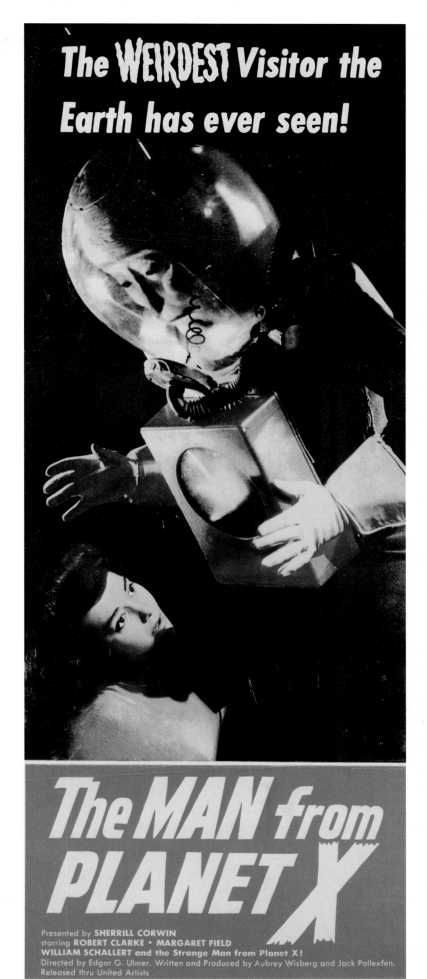

The WEIRDEST Visitor the Earth has ever seen!

The MAN from PLANET X

Presented by SHERRILL CORWIN
starring ROBERT CLARKE · MARGARET FIELD
WILLIAM SCHALLERT and the Strange Man from Planet X!
Directed by Edgar G. Ulmer. Written and Produced by Aubrey Wisberg and Jack Pollexfen.
Released thru United Artists

3. MAN FROM PLANET X, 1951, insert

STRANGE POWER FROM ANOTHER PLANET MENACES THE EARTH !

THE DAY THE EARTH STOOD STILL

WITH
MICHAEL RENNIE
PATRICIA NEAL
HUGH MARLOWE
PRODUCED BY JULIAN BLAUSTEIN · DIRECTED BY ROBERT WISE
SCREEN PLAY BY EDMUND H. NORTH

4. THE DAY THE EARTH STOOD STILL, 1951, insert

FROM OUT OF SPACE.....
A WARNING AND AN ULTIMATUM!

THE DAY THE EARTH STOOD STILL

MICHAEL RENNIE · PATRICIA NEAL · HUGH MARLOWE · JULIAN BLAUSTEIN · ROBERT WISE · EDMUND H. NORTH

5. THE DAY THE EARTH STOOD STILL, 1951, window card

ROCKET 180,000,000 YEARS INTO THE UNKNOWN!

Lost Continent

CESAR ROMERO
Hillary BROOKE · Chick CHANDLER · John HOYT · Sid MELTON
ACQUANETTA

Lost Continent
CESAR ROMERO

6. THE LOST CONTINENT, 1951, lobby cards

7. THE THING, 1951, one-sheet

8. CAT-WOMEN OF THE MOON, 1953, lobby cards

9. BELA LUGOSI MEETS A BROOKLYN GORILLA, 1952, lobby cards

10. RED PLANET MARS UNFOLDED, 1952, half-sheet

11. INVADERS FROM MARS, 1953, one-sheet

12. IT CAME FROM OUTER SPACE, 1953, one-sheet

13. ROBOT MONSTER, 1953, one-sheet

14. PHANTOM FROM SPACE, 1953, one-sheet

15. PROJECT MOONBASE, 1953, lobby cards

16. GOG, 1954, lobby cards

A MILLION CENTURIES OF FURY RAGES UP FROM THE AMAZON'S FORBIDDEN DEPTHS!

BLACK LAGOON

(front)

YOU sail the Amazon's uncharted waters!

YOU swim through a world unseen by human eyes!

YOU witness a death struggle in the deep!

YOU are trapped in the grotto of the Black Lagoon!

Produced in U.I.'s Success-tradition to follow in the BOX OFFICE foot steps of "FRANKENSTEIN," "THE WOLF MAN"..."PHANTOM OF THE OPERA"..."DRACULA"

UNIVERSAL-INTERNATIONAL presents

CREATURE FROM THE Black Lagoon

STARRING **RICHARD CARLSON** • **JULIA ADAMS**

with RICHARD DENNING • ANTONIO MORENO • NESTOR PAIVA • WHIT BISSELL

Directed by JACK ARNOLD • Screenplay by HARRY ESSEX and ARTHUR ROSS • Story by MAURICE ZIMM • Produced by WILLIAM ALLAND

(back)

TERRIFYING CREATURE FROM A LOST AGE

every man his mortal enemy... and woman's beauty prey for his strange passions!

AVAILABLE IN BOTH 3D AND 2D

CREATURE FROM THE BLACK LAGOON

(interior)

17. CREATURE FROM THE BLACK LAGOON, 1954, special promo brochure

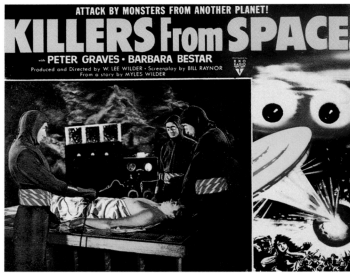

18. TOBOR THE GREAT, 1954, lobby cards

19. KILLERS FROM SPACE, 1954, lobby cards

20. MONSTER FROM THE OCEAN FLOOR, 1954, one-sheet

21. PHANTOM OF THE RUE MORGUE, 1954, one-sheet

22. RIDERS TO THE STARS, 1954, lobby cards

23. TARGET EARTH, 1954, one-sheet

24. THEM, 1954, one-sheet

25. DEVIL GIRL FROM MARS, 1955, lobby cards

26. THIS ISLAND, EARTH, 1955, one-sheet

27. THIS ISLAND, EARTH, 1955, lobby cards

28. THE BEAST WITH 1,000,000 EYES, 1955, one-sheet

29. IT CAME FROM BENEATH THE SEA, 1955, one-sheet

30. CULT OF THE COBRA, 1955, lobby cards

31. REVENGE OF THE CREATURE, 1955, half-sheet

32. REVENGE OF THE CREATURE, 1955, lobby cards

33. TARANTULA, 1955, one-sheet

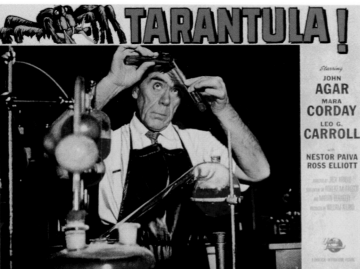

34. TARANTULA, 1955, lobby cards

35. CREATURE WITH THE ATOM BRAIN, 1955,
one-sheet

36. KING DINOSAUR, 1955, lobby cards

37. SVENGALI, 1955, lobby cards

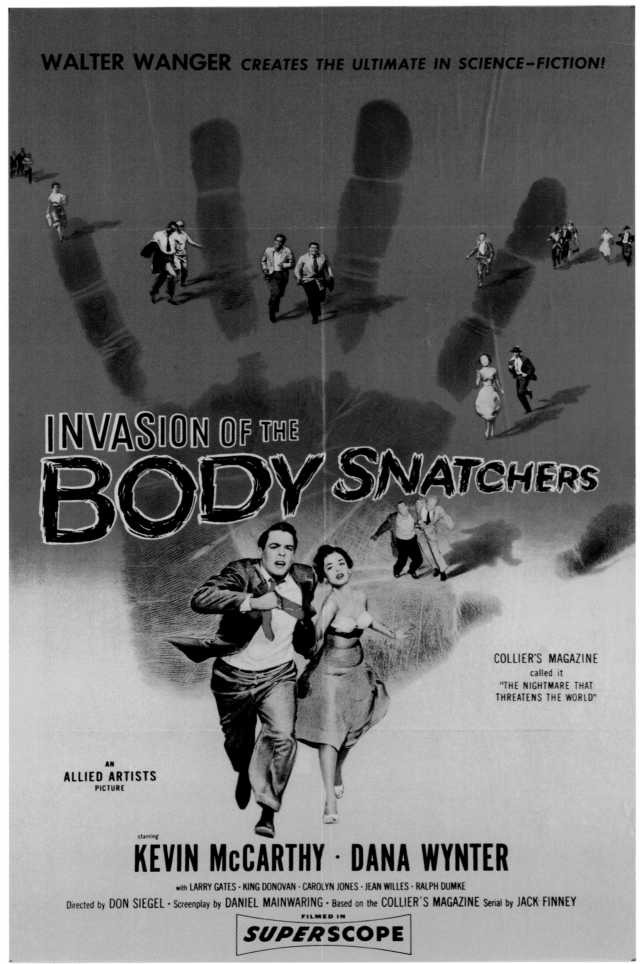

38. INVASION OF THE BODY SNATCHERS, 1956, one-sheet

39. INVASION OF THE BODY SNATCHERS, 1956, lobby cards

40. ON THE THRESHOLD OF SPACE, 1956,
lobby cards

41. THE CREEPING UNKNOWN, 1956,
lobby cards

42. WORLD WITHOUT END, 1956, lobby cards

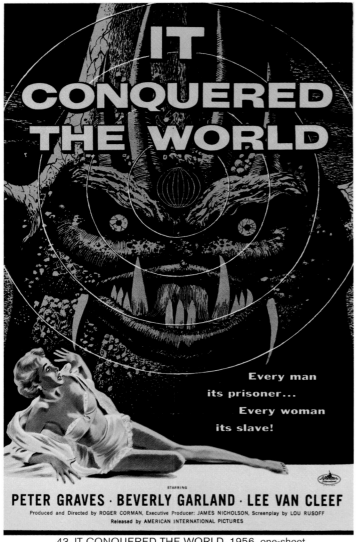

43. IT CONQUERED THE WORLD, 1956, one-sheet

44. DAY THE WORLD ENDED, 1956, one-sheet

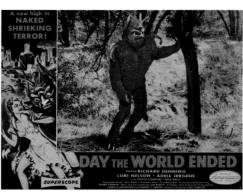

45. DAY THE WORLD ENDED, 1956, lobby cards

46. DAY THE WORLD ENDED, 1956, half-sheet

47. THE CREATURE WALKS AMONG US, 1956, one-sheet

48. THE CREATURE WALKS AMONG US, 1956, lobby cards

49. INDESTRUCTIBLE MAN, 1956, lobby cards

50. THE ATOMIC MAN, 1956, lobby cards

51. THE BEAST OF HOLLOW MOUNTAIN, 1956, lobby cards

52. EARTH VS. THE FLYING SAUCERS, 1956, one-sheet

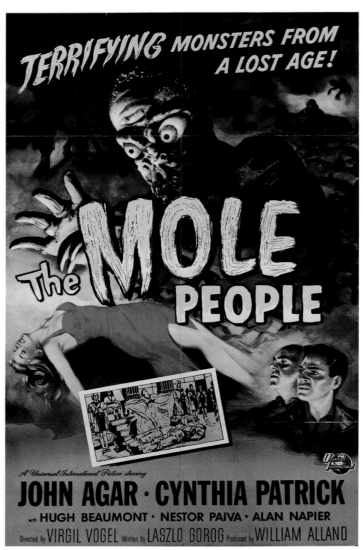

53. THE MOLE PEOPLE, 1956, one-sheet

54. THE SHE-CREATURE, 1956, lobby cards

55. THE SHE-CREATURE, 1956, half-sheet

56. THE BLACK SLEEP, 1956, lobby cards

57. BRIDE OF THE MONSTER, 1956, lobby cards

58. BRIDE OF THE MONSTER, 1956, insert

59. GODZILLA KING OF THE MONSTERS, 1956, one-sheet

60. GODZILLA KING OF THE MONSTERS, 1956, half-sheet

61. PHARAOH'S CURSE, 1956, lobby cards

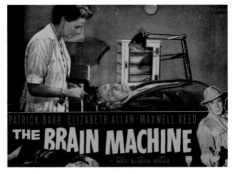

62. THE BRAIN MACHINE, 1956, lobby cards

63. FIRE MAIDENS OF OUTER SPACE, 1956, lobby cards

64. FORBIDDEN PLANET, 1956, one-sheet

65. FORBIDDEN PLANET, 1956, lobby cards

66. THE WEREWOLF, 1956, lobby cards

67. THE PHANTOM FROM 10,000 LEAGUES,
1956, lobby cards

68. HALF HUMAN, 1957, lobby cards

69. RODAN, 1956, lobby cards

70. 20 MILLION MILES TO EARTH, 1957, lobby cards

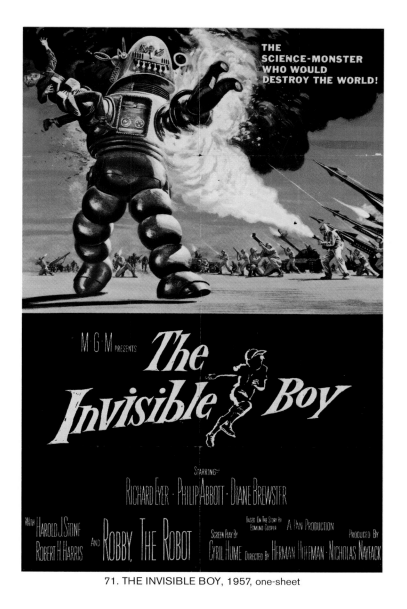

71. THE INVISIBLE BOY, 1957, one-sheet

72. THE INVISIBLE BOY, 1957, lobby cards

73. THE UNDEAD, 1957, lobby cards

74. KRONOS, 1957, lobby cards

75. MONSTER FROM GREEN HELL, 1957, lobby cards

76. THE MONOLITH MONSTERS, 1957, one-sheet

77. THE ASTOUNDING SHE-MONSTER, 1957, one-sheet

78. MONOLITH MONSTERS, 1957, lobby cards

79. ATTACK OF THE CRAB MONSTERS, 1957, lobby cards

80. THE ASTOUNDING SHE MONSTER, 1957, lobby cards

81. I WAS A TEENAGE FRANKENSTEIN, 1957, lobby cards

82. THE CURSE OF FRANKENSTEIN, 1957, one-sheet

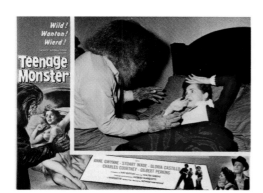

83. TEENAGE MONSTER, 1957, lobby cards

84. THE CAT GIRL, 1957, lobby cards

85. THE VAMPIRE, 1957, lobby cards

86. ATTACK OF THE CRAB
MONSTERS, 1957, insert

87. NOT OF THIS EARTH, 1957, lobby cards

88. FROM HELL IT CAME, 1957, lobby cards

89. THE NIGHT THE WORLD EXPLODED,
1957, lobby cards

90. UNKNOWN TERROR, 1957, lobby cards

91. I WAS A TEENAGE WEREWOLF, 1957, one-sheet

92. I WAS A TEENAGE WEREWOLF, 1957, lobby cards

93. BLOOD OF DRACULA, 1957, lobby cards

94. DAUGHTER OF DR. JEKYLL, 1957, lobby cards

95. THE CYCLOPS, 1957, lobby cards

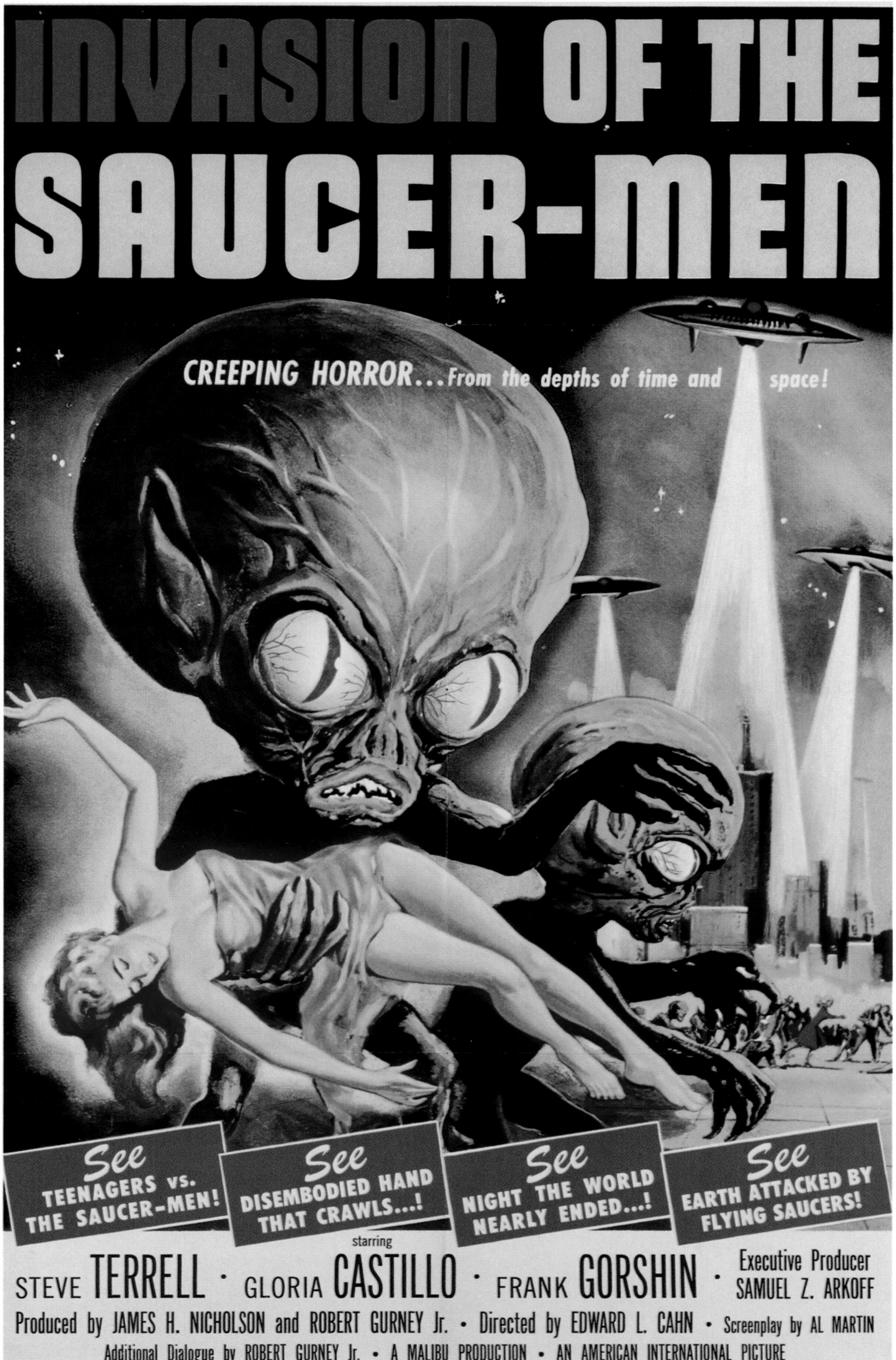

96. INVASION OF THE SAUCER-MEN, 1957, one-sheet

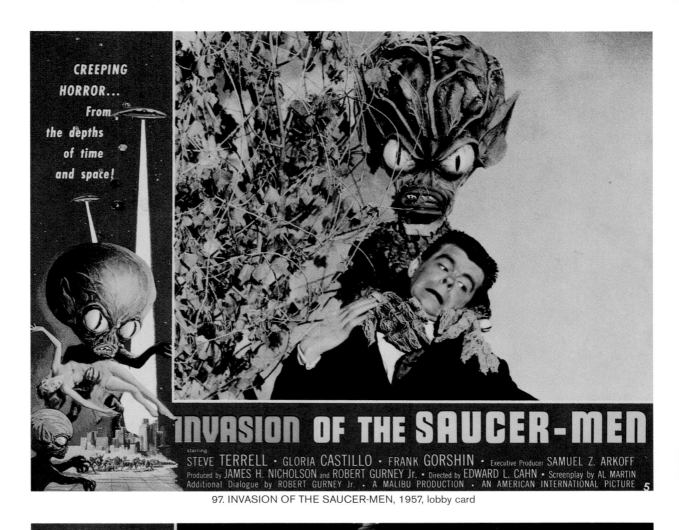

97. INVASION OF THE SAUCER-MEN, 1957, lobby card

98. INVASION OF THE SAUCER-MEN, 1957, lobby card

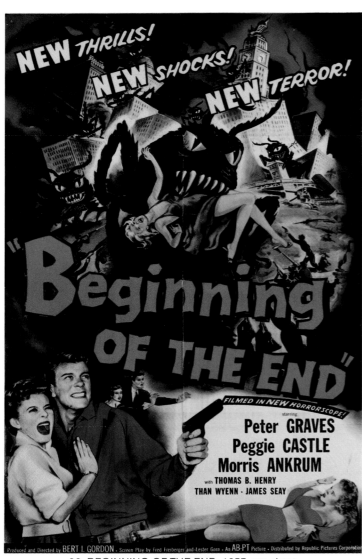

99. BEGINNING OF THE END, 1957, one-sheet

100. BEGINNING OF THE END, 1957, lobby cards

101. THE UNEARTHLY, 1957, lobby cards

102. SHE DEVIL, 1957, lobby cards

103. THE LAND UNKNOWN, 1957, lobby cards

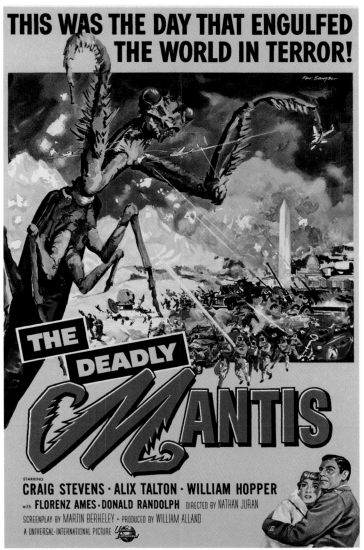

104. THE DEADLY MANTIS, 1957, one-sheet

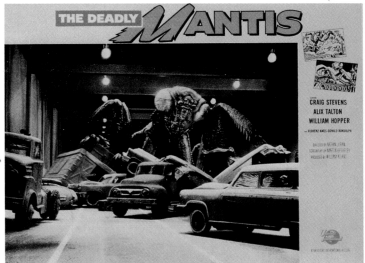

105. THE DEADLY MANTIS, 1957, lobby cards

106. THE DEADLY MANTIS, 1957, insert

107. THE MAN WHO TURNED TO STONE, 1957, one-sheet

108. THE MAN WHO TURNED TO STONE, 1957, lobby cards

109. THE BLACK SCORPION, 1957, lobby cards

110. THE GIANT CLAW, 1957, lobby cards

111. VOODOO WOMAN, 1957, lobby cards

112. VOODOO ISLAND, 1957, one-sheet

113. ZOMBIES OF MORA TAU, 1957, lobby cards

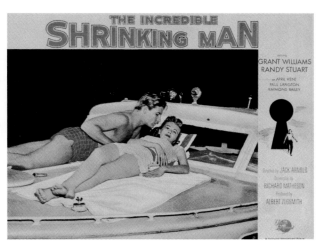

114. THE INCREDIBLE SHRINKING MAN, 1957, lobby cards

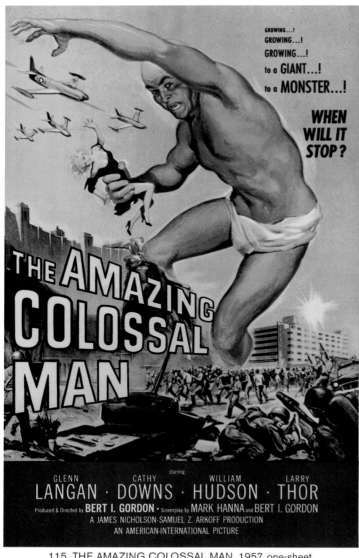

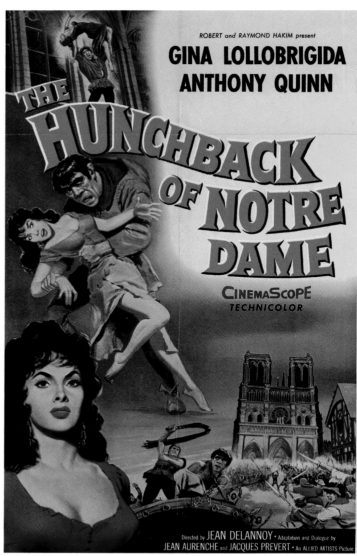

115. THE AMAZING COLOSSAL MAN, 1957, one-sheet

116. THE HUNCHBACK OF NOTRE DAME, 1957, one-sheet

117. THE BRAIN FROM THE PLANET AROUS, 1957, lobby cards

118. BACK FROM THE DEAD, 1957, lobby cards

119. THE ABOMINABLE SNOWMAN OF THE HIMALAYAS, 1957, lobby cards

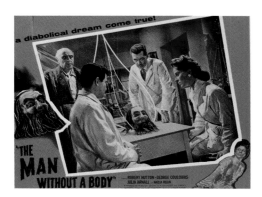

120. THE MAN WITHOUT A BODY, 1957,
lobby cards

121. NIGHT OF THE BLOOD BEAST, 1958,
lobby cards

122. MONSTER ON THE CAMPUS, 1958,
lobby cards

123. COSMIC MONSTERS, 1958, one-sheet

124. COSMIC MONSTERS, 1958, lobby cards

125. THE BRIDE AND THE BEAST, 1958, one-sheet

126. THE BRIDE AND THE BEAST, 1958, lobby cards

127. GIANT FROM THE UNKNOWN, 1958,
lobby cards

128. SHE DEMONS, 1958, lobby cards

129. TEENAGE CAVEMAN, 1958, lobby cards

130. I MARRIED A MONSTER FROM OUTER SPACE, 1958, lobby cards

131. MACABRE, 1958, lobby cards

132. SCREAMING SKULL, 1958, lobby cards

133. TERROR IN THE HAUNTED HOUSE, 1958, lobby cards

134. THE MONSTER THAT CHALLENGED THE WORLD, 1957, lobby cards

135. ATTACK OF THE 50 FT. WOMAN, 1958, lobby cards

136. ATTACK OF THE 50 FT. WOMAN, 1958, one-sheet

137. IT! THE TERROR FROM BEYOND SPACE, 1958, one-sheet

138. IT! THE TERROR FROM BEYOND SPACE, 1958, lobby cards

139. THE LOST MISSILE, 1958, lobby cards

140. WAR OF THE SATELLITES, 1958, lobby cards

141. SPACE MASTER X-7, 1958, lobby cards

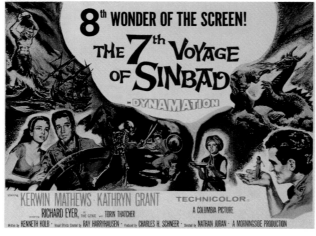

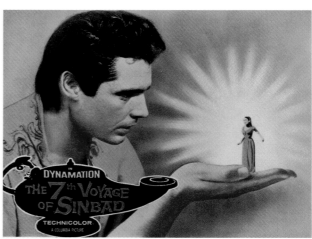

142. THE 7TH VOYAGE OF SINBAD, 1958, lobby cards

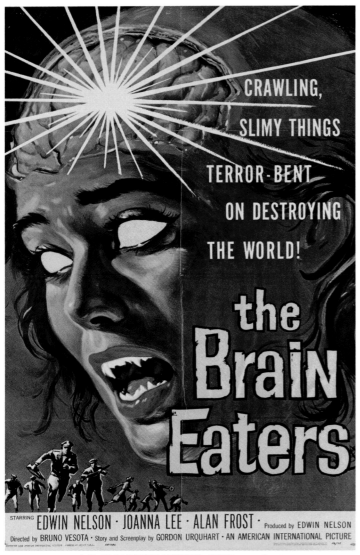

143. THE BRAIN EATERS, 1958, one-sheet

144. THE SPIDER, 1958, one-sheet

145. BLOOD OF THE VAMPIRE, 1958, lobby cards

146. TERROR FROM THE YEAR 5,000, 1958, lobby cards

147. FRANKENSTEIN'S DAUGHTER, 1958, lobby cards

148. THE BLOB, 1958, one-sheet

149. THE BLOB, 1958, lobby cards

150. HORROR OF DRACULA, 1958, half-sheet

151. THE RETURN OF DRACULA, 1958,
lobby cards

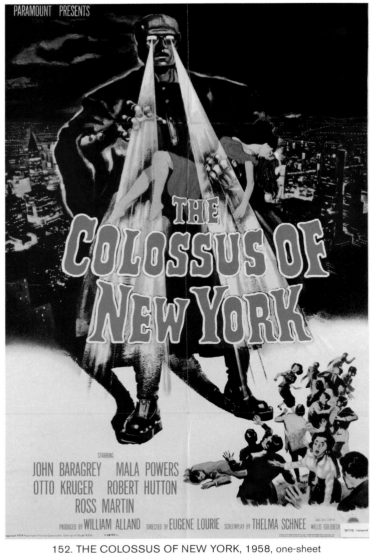

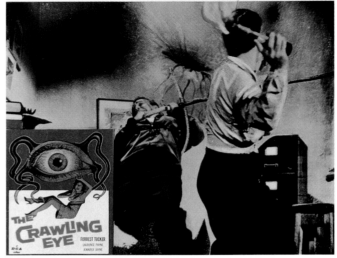

152. THE COLOSSUS OF NEW YORK, 1958, one-sheet

153. THE CRAWLING EYE, 1958, lobby cards

154. THE SPACE CHILDREN, 1958, lobby cards

155. ATTACK OF THE PUPPET PEOPLE, 1958, lobby cards

156. VIKING WOMEN AND THE SEA SERPENT, 1958, lobby cards

157. MISSILE TO THE MOON, 1958, lobby cards

158. THE FLY, 1958, one-sheet

159. THE FLY, 1958, lobby cards

160. QUEEN OF OUTER SPACE, 1958, lobby cards

161. THE MYSTERIANS, 1959, lobby cards

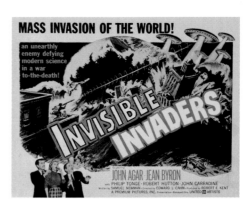

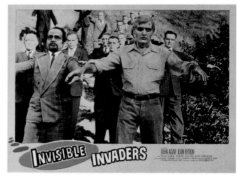

162. THE ANGRY RED PLANET, 1960,
lobby cards

163. THE H MAN, 1959, lobby cards

164. INVISIBLE INVADERS, 1959, lobby cards

165. THE ALLIGATOR PEOPLE, 1959, lobby cards

166. 4D MAN, 1959, lobby cards

THE BIGGEST THING SINCE CREATION!

The GIANT
BEHEMOTH

An ALLIED ARTISTS Picture

starring GENE EVANS · ANDRE MORELL · JOHN TURNER · A DAVID DIAMOND PRODUCTION
Directed by EUGENE LOURIE · Screenplay by EUGENE LOURIE · Special Effects Designed and Created by JACK RABIN · IRVING BLOCK · LOUIS DE WITT

167. THE GIANT BEHEMOTH, 1959, one-sheet

168. THE GIANT BEHEMOTH, 1959, lobby cards

169. TEENAGE ZOMBIES, 1959, lobby cards

170. THE GIANT GILA MONSTER, 1959, lobby cards

171. ATTACK OF THE JUNGLE WOMAN, 1959, lobby cards

172. CURSE OF THE UNDEAD, 1959,
lobby cards

173. THE HEAD, 1959, lobby cards

174. BLACK PIT OF DR. M, 1959, lobby cards

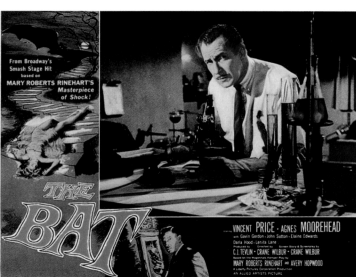

175. THE BAT, 1959, lobby cards

176. A BUCKET OF BLOOD, 1959, lobby cards

177. THE MUMMY, 1959, one-sheet

178. THE MUMMY, 1959, lobby cards

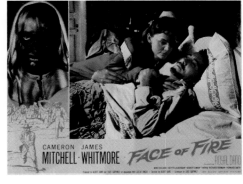

179. HORRORS OF THE BLACK MUSEUM,
1959, lobby cards

180. FACE OF FIRE, 1959, lobby cards

181. FOUR SKULLS OF JONATHAN DRAKE,
1959, lobby cards

182. BEAST FROM HAUNTED CAVE, 1959,
lobby cards

183. GIGANTIS THE FIRE MONSTER, 1959,
lobby cards

184. RETURN OF THE FLY, 1959, lobby cards

185. THE GIANT LEECHES, 1959, lobby cards

186. HIDEOUS SUN DEMON, 1959, one-sheet

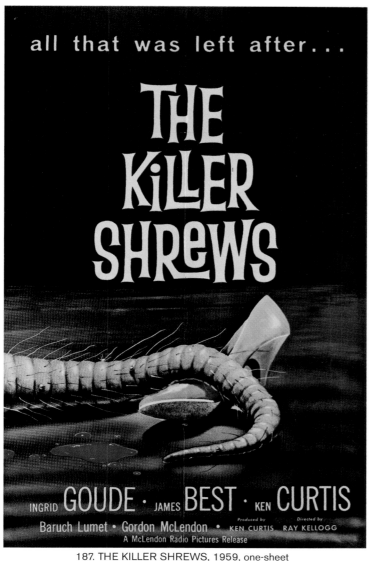

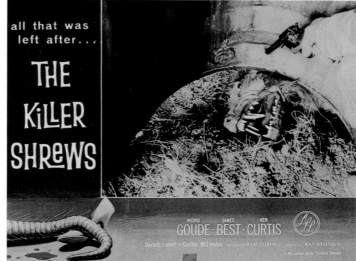

187. THE KILLER SHREWS, 1959, one-sheet

188. THE KILLER SHREWS, 1959, lobby cards

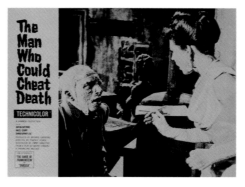

189. THE AMAZING TRANSPARENT MAN,
1959, lobby cards

190. THE MAN WHO COULD CHEAT DEATH,
1959, lobby cards

191. GHOST OF DRAGSTRIP HOLLOW,
1959, lobby cards

192. JOURNEY TO THE CENTER OF THE EARTH, 1959, lobby cards

193. THE WASP WOMAN, 1959, one-sheet

194. THE WASP WOMAN, 1959, lobby cards

195. BRIDES OF DRACULA, 1960, lobby cards

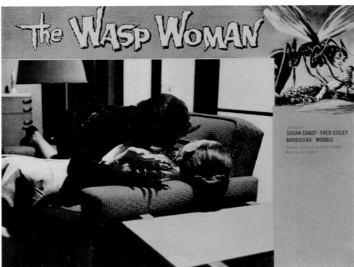

196. THE LEECH WOMAN, 1960, lobby cards

197. HOUSE OF USHER, 1960, lobby cards

198. HOUSE OF FRIGHT, 1960, lobby cards

199. VILLAGE OF THE DAMNED, 1960, one-sheet

200. VILLAGE OF THE DAMNED, 1960, lobby cards

201. MACUMBA LOVE, 1960, lobby cards

202. CIRCUS OF HORRORS, 1960, one-sheet

203. CIRCUS OF HORRORS, 1960, lobby cards

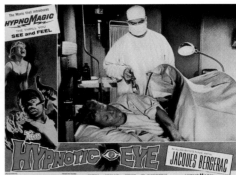

204. ELECTRONIC MONSTER, 1960,
lobby cards

205. HYPNOTIC EYE, 1960, lobby cards

206. THE ANGRY RED PLANET, 1960, one-sheet

207. CALTIKI THE IMMORTAL MONSTER, 1960, one-sheet

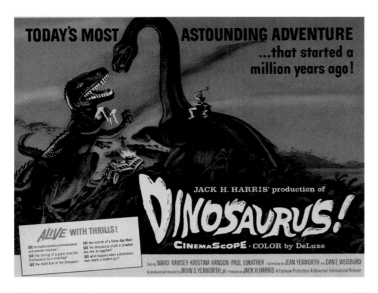

208. DINOSAURUS, 1960, lobby cards

209. 13 GHOSTS, 1960, lobby cards

210. THE LOST WORLD, 1960, lobby cards

211. BATTLE IN OUTER SPACE, 1960, lobby cards

212. 12 TO THE MOON, 1960, lobby cards

213. THE TIME MACHINE, 1960, lobby cards

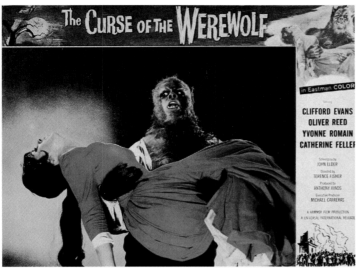

214. THE CURSE OF THE WEREWOLF, 1960, lobby cards

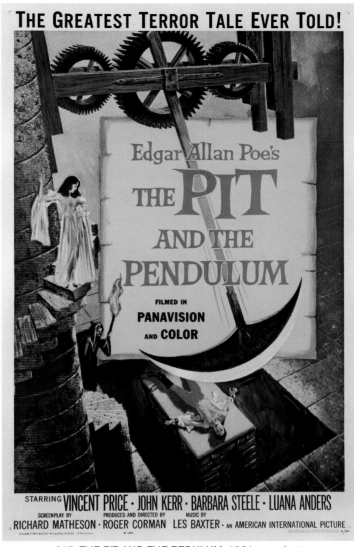

215. THE PIT AND THE PEDULUM, 1961, one-sheet

216. THE DEAD ONE, 1960, lobby cards

217. PRISONER OF THE IRON MASK, 1961,
lobby cards

218. BURN WITCH BURN, 1962, lobby cards

219. THE MINOTAUR, 1961, lobby cards

220. THE SHADOW OF THE CAT, 1961,
lobby cards

221. VALLEY OF THE DRAGONS, 1961,
lobby cards

222, GORGO, 1961, one-sheet

223. GORGO, 1961, lobby cards

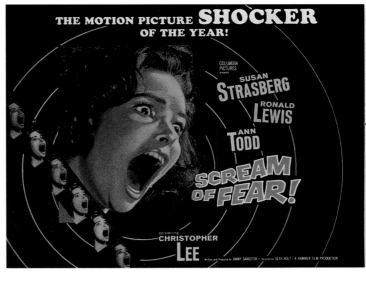

224. MR. SARDONICUS, 1961, lobby cards

225. SCREAM OF FEAR, 1961, lobby cards

226. JOURNEY TO THE SEVENTH PLANET, 1961, lobby cards

227. MASTER OF THE WORLD, 1961, lobby cards

228. THE DAY THE SKY EXPLODED, 1961, lobby cards

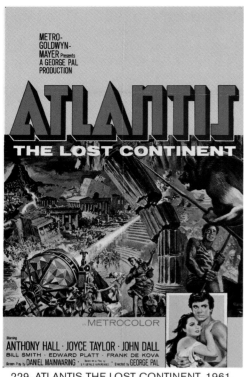

229. ATLANTIS THE LOST CONTINENT, 1961,
one-sheet

230. ATLANTIS THE LOST CONTINENT, 1961,
lobby cards

231. CREATURE FROM THE HAUNTED SEA,
1961, lobby cards

232. BLACK SUNDAY, 1961, lobby cards

233. BLOOD AND ROSES, 1961, lobby cards

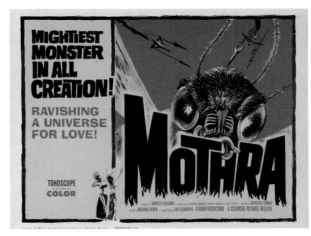

234. MOTHRA, 1962, lobby cards

235. MOTHRA, 1962, half-sheet

236. PANIC IN YEAR ZERO, 1962, lobby cards

237. HAND OF DEATH, 1962, lobby cards

238. INVASION OF THE ANIMAL PEOPLE, 1962, lobby cards

239. THE PHANTOM OF THE OPERA, 1962, lobby cards

240. TALES OF TERROR, 1962, lobby cards

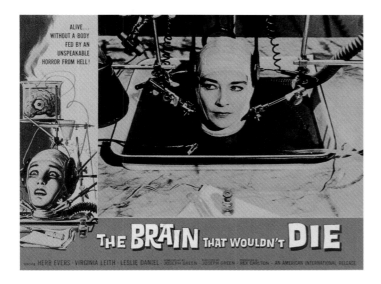

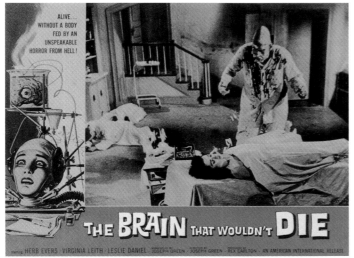

241. THE BRAIN THAT WOULDN'T DIE, 1962, lobby cards

242. THE PREMATURE BURIAL, 1962, lobby cards

243. THE VAMPIRE AND THE BALLERINA,
1962, lobby cards

244. DOCTOR BLOOD'S COFFIN, 1961,
lobby cards

245. THE TELL-TALE HEART, 1962, lobby cards

246. THE PHANTOM PLANET, 1962, lobby cards

247. ASSIGNMENT OUTER-SPACE, 1962, lobby cards

248. BATTLE BEYOND THE SUN, 1962, lobby cards

249. FIRST SPACESHIP ON VENUS, 1962, lobby cards

250. THE DAY OF THE TRIFFIDS, 1962, lobby cards

251. VARAN THE UNBELIEVABLE, 1962, lobby cards

252. KING KONG VS. GODZILLA, 1963, one-sheet

253. BEAUTY AND THE BEAST, 1962,
lobby cards

254. EEGAH, 1962, lobby cards

255. HERCULES AND THE CAPTIVE
WOMEN, 1963, lobby cards

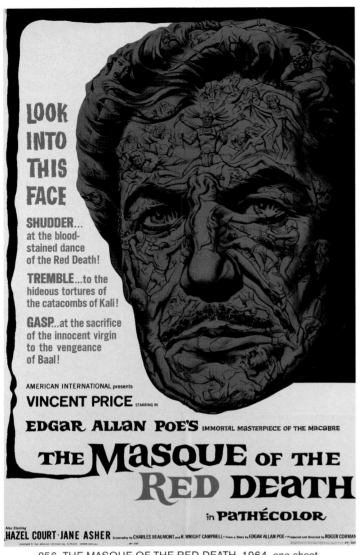

256. THE MASQUE OF THE RED DEATH, 1964, one-sheet

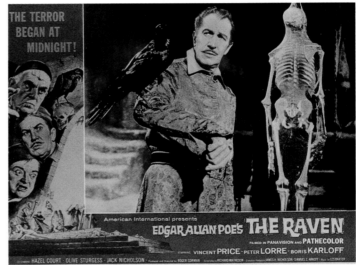

257. THE RAVEN, 1963, lobby cards

258. DEMENTIA 13, 1963, lobby cards

259. MILL OF THE STONE WOMEN, 1963,
lobby cards

260. NIGHT TIDE, 1963, lobby cards

WHO GOES THERE? INDEX

WHO GOES THERE? INDEX